PRAISE FOR

SEX AND INTIMACY FOR WOUNDED VETERANS

"Tastefully Illustrated, *Sex and Intimacy for Wounded Veterans* is a one-of-a-kind position and device resource, especially for anyone who has experienced limb loss or serious genital injury."

—Mitchell Tepper, PHD, MPH, author of *Regain That Feeling: Secrets to Sexual Self-Discovery*

"Veterans and spouses often describe difficulty with sexual intimacy as their greatest hurdle to healing, while doctors and therapists frequently describe sex as the issue they are most unprepared to address. In *Sex and Intimacy for Wounded Veterans: A Guide to Embracing Change*, both veterans and health care workers will find a comprehensive and compassionate guide. We should put a copy of this manual in the hands of every patient, spouse, and medical provider who walks through the door of a Military Treatment Facility."

—Emilie E. Godwin, Ph.D., LPC, MFT, Assistant Professor and Director of Psychotherapy & Family Services, Virginia Commonwealth University Neuropsychology—Traumatic Brain Injury Model System of Care

SEX AND INTIMACY

FOR WOUNDED VETERANS

A GUIDE TO EMBRACING CHANGE

Kathryn Ellis, MOT, OTR/L and
Caitlin Dennison, MOT, OTR/L

Sex and Intimacy for Wounded Veterans: A Guide to Embracing Change
By Kathryn Ellis, MOT, OTR/L and Caitlin Dennison, MOT, OTR/L

ISBN-13: 978-0-9862679-6-3
ISBN-10: 0986267961

Illustrations and Cover Illustrated by Liza Biggers
Cover Designed by Siori Kitajima, SF AppWorks LLC
http://www.sfappworks.com
Formatting by Siori Kitajima for SF AppWorks LLC
E-Book Formatted by Ovidiu Vlad
Book and E-book published by The Sager Group LLC
info@TheSagerGroup.net
This book contains explicit content not suitable for children.

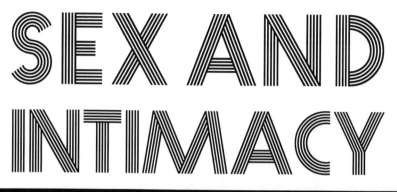

SEX AND INTIMACY

FOR WOUNDED VETERANS

A GUIDE TO EMBRACING CHANGE

Kathryn Ellis, MOT, OTR/L and
Caitlin Dennison, MOT, OTR/L

THE SAGER GROUP

Artifex Te Adiuva

TABLE OF CONTENTS

INTRODUCTION

Human contact and sexuality are natural and essential parts of our lives. Sexual need and desire do not dissipate when someone has experienced traumatic injuries. While you may be experiencing a number of changes due to your injuries, it does not mean that sexual activity and intimacy are not possible. On the contrary, the very changes you experience could present new opportunities for you and your partner. To help you in discovering the possibilities, this manual was created to serve as a starting point to provide information and resources about re-engaging in sexual activity and intimacy, with or without adaptations and modifications.

Written by occupational therapists who work with wounded service members, the manual is designed to educate service members, veterans, families, significant others, and clinicians regarding sexual health following injury. Certain diagnoses considered in creating this manual include but are not limited to: traumatic brain injury (TBI), post-traumatic stress disorder (PTSD), genital injuries, spinal cord injury (SCI), and orthopedic injuries involving muscles, bones, nerves, and limb amputations. Regardless of injury, sexual pleasure with yourself or with a partner is a realistic goal, as is the ability to form intimate relationships with others.

After, or as you read the manual, you are encouraged to talk with your medical team and occupational therapist (OT) about any questions you might have and work together to complete a comprehensive activity analysis for your resumed sexual activity and intimacy. An activity analysis is a comprehensive breakdown of a task, establishing the cognitive, physical, and emotional requirements to complete a task, as well as establishing suggestions, treatments, and modifications necessary for a person to succeed at the activity. Your occupational therapist has been specifically trained to assist in restoring a patient's ability to perform his or her activities of daily living (ADLs), which include self-care such as feeding, toileting, and dressing, as well as higher-level activities such as home maintenance, driving, work, managing intimate relationships and sexual activity.

DISCLAIMER

The information in this manual is not intended to be medical advice or to provide suggestions applicable to everyone. The devices and ideas discussed in this manual are not specific recommendations; rather, they are general examples to provide information to a large group with varying injuries. The authors were not solicited or compensated by the manufacturers of the products in this manual. No endorsement is explicit or implied. This information reflects the opinions of the authors as occupational therapists and not the opinion of the authors' place of employment or sponsors of the manual.

WARNING

The authors and those involved in the production of the manual do not take responsibility for any harm or injury caused by using any technique or device mentioned in this manual. Always ask questions of health care providers and take into consideration specific individual abilities, risks, and benefits regarding those activities that can be safely performed.

HEALTH CARE PROFESSIONALS WHO ADDRESS SEXUAL HEALTH

Health care professionals who address sexual health include but are not limited to: primary care physicians, urologists, gynecologists, behavioral health providers (psychologists, psychiatrists, social workers), occupational therapists, nurses, fertility specialists, peer counselors, certified sexuality educators, certified sexuality counselors, and certified sex therapists.

CHAPTER 1

WHAT IS SEXUAL HEALTH AND INTIMACY?

Sexual health is a state of physical, emotional, mental, and social well-being related to sexuality (erotic desires, practices, and identity). It involves being sexually active with yourself or a partner and effectively communicating sexual needs and desires.

Intimacy means having a close, personal, familiar, affectionate, loving relationship with another person or group with whom there is shared knowledge and understanding. Having an emotional and/or physical component, intimacy improves your health and your relationships with your family and others.

Both sexual health and intimacy allow you to resume, establish, and strengthen relationships that provide pleasure, comfort, and emotional support.

CHAPTER 2

DIAGNOSES COMMON TO WOUNDED SERVICE MEMBERS

Regardless of the nature of injury, it is crucial to keep the lines of communication open with a partner when engaging in sexual activity. This will help to foster emotional intimacy and trust. Open communication is important before, during, and after sexual activity to ensure both partners are comfortable, especially if something is new for either partner or a suggestion to a partner is being made. The most effective time to discuss issues, concerns, or suggested improvements is when both partners are clothed and sexual activity is not about to occur and has not just occurred. Use foreplay and after-play as times to be loving and intimate and to enjoy each other's touch and pleasure instead of providing specific concerns or suggestions. Physical, emotional, and cognitive trauma can result when there is difficulty with intimate communication and can add stress to a relationship. Showing patience, listening, and being respectful and receptive to a partner's input can lead to greater satisfaction for both partners.

TBI

Traumatic brain injuries occur to varying degrees: mild, moderate, severe, and penetrating. It is possible to notice physical, cognitive, and emotional changes at any severity of TBI, which may or may not affect sexuality and intimacy. Communication with a sexual partner regarding sexual desires and challenges can improve sexual satisfaction for both partners. Also, discussing noted challenges with a health care provider can improve access to education and support. An occupational therapist can suggest coping strategies for improving memory, planning and organizing for a sexual activity alone or with a partner, and developing skills to initiate or enhance an intimate and trusting relationship. For example, scheduling sex for a time when individuals typically have the most energy and in a location with the least distractions can facilitate performance and a better sexual atmosphere. Also, creating a separate space designated for sex and intimacy can be helpful if areas, such as bedrooms and bathrooms, are typically for caregiving activities and filled with durable medical equipment. A spare bedroom, basement, or den can be a designated space for sex and intimacy, and that room can be filled with items that invoke eroticism and desire.

A TBI can also cause significant physical impairments related to tone, motor planning, and fine motor skills. Hemiplegia is when a part of the body is paralyzed, and hemiparesis is when a part of the body is weaker and motor planning is possible, but difficult. Both can be caused by a TBI. An occupational therapist can assist by focusing on return of fine motor skills in therapy, and/or suggesting toys and ways to attach them to arms that have limited grasp and fine motor skills. Chapter 6 provides general positioning options, while an occupational therapist can suggest specific suggestions about positioning or aides.

PTSD

Post-traumatic stress disorder is an anxiety disorder resulting in high stress levels that have an impact on participation and satisfaction in life activities, including sex and intimacy. Communication with a sexual partner regarding needs, triggers, sexual desires, and challenges can improve sexual satisfaction for both partners. Also, discussing noted challenges with a health care provider can assist with improved access to education and support. For example, a health care provider might suggest tantric breathing exercises to calm stress and worries and to enhance sexual experience. In addition, adjustments in timing and location may provide a more conducive sexual atmosphere.

Orthopedic Injuries

Orthopedic injuries include muscular, bone, and nerve injuries resulting in loss of movement, loss of limbs, and increased pain. External fixators and splints are typically used to heal orthopedic injuries and can limit movement. Upper and lower prosthetics can change how an activity is performed. Movement limitations can create challenges for positioning, masturbation, and pleasuring partners through touch. Having open communication with your sexual partner; discussing positioning with your therapists; or reviewing the modifications and adaptations, positioning aids, equipment, and devices, and positioning tips highlighted in this manual can all assist with improving performance and satisfaction.

Spinal Cord Injuries

Spinal cord injuries are any injury to the spinal cord or nerve endings at the end of the spinal cord resulting in changes in sensation, strength, and body functions. These changes occur below the spinal cord level affected by the injury—higher up the spinal cord, more of the body will be affected by sensory, strength, and/or function loss. The nerve injury can be complete or incomplete, which will determine the combination of sensation, strength, and/or function affected. Spinal cord injury can result in limitations for full body movement, fine motor skills of the hands and arms, sensation of body parts including genitals, and functioning of body systems, such as genital, bowel, and bladder functions. Education and engaging in physical and occupational therapy after spinal cord injury is important for developing a plan for self-care, such as toileting, dressing, and bathing, and improving independence with mobility, such as learning to propel a wheelchair. Discussion with a urologist or spinal cord injury nurse educator regarding sexual abilities will provide realistic expectations for sexual performance. Discussion with an occupational therapist regarding positioning aides, sexual devices, and how to communicate sexual desires and goals with a partner can provide insight into alternative ways to achieve sex positions and sexual pleasure for yourself and partner. Communicating with a partner regarding realistic expectations, as well as preferred sexual activities and enjoyment will enhance the likelihood of pleasurable sexual experiences and reduce the effects of physical limitations on sexual enjoyment.

Paralyzed Veterans of America is an organization that provides comprehensive educational information for those with a spinal cord injury through free downloadable guides. "Sexuality and Reproductive Health for Adults with Spinal Cord Injury: What You Should Know" is a specific guide providing accurate sexual health education and suggestions to improve sexual performance. Visit www.PVA.org to locate this publication.

Genital injuries

Genital injuries can include skin injuries of testicles, penis, or surrounding area; partial or complete loss of external genitals; nerve or spinal cord injury affecting reproductive/urinary systems; and internal injuries to reproductive/urinary system. Urology can assist with providing information regarding the impact of each specific injury on sexual function and reproduction, as well as when it is safe to engage in sexual activity. Reviewing sex toys and/or discussing your desires and challenges with a health care professional can assist with providing suggestions for alternative ways to achieve sexual pleasure. Scar tissue massage, exploring other erogenous zones, and using sex toys can help return sexual satisfaction. Certain sex positions can continue to stimulate a partner, such as positioning male partner on top while he uses his pelvic bone to stimulate a partner's clitoris. Loss of testicles and penis does not imply loss of ability to ejaculate, and loss of ability to ejaculate does not imply loss of ability to orgasm. Orgasm can be achieved in other ways, including through stimulation to nipples and other erogenous zones, as well as psychological stimulation. As always, communication with a sexual partner is highly encouraged to provide awareness of partner's concerns and desires and to facilitate discussion regarding how to enhance the sexual experience for both partners.

CHAPTER 3

GENERAL TIPS FOR ENGAGING IN INTIMACY

Individuals often experience multiple injuries that can affect sexual health and intimacy. In chapter 2 the following diagnoses were discussed: amputations, TBI, PTSD, SCI, orthopedic injuries, and genital injuries. Often these diagnoses can create challenges to maintaining intimacy, because accepting the injury often takes priority. However, with education, partner communication, problem solving, and an open mind, intimacy and sexual activity can be experienced and enjoyed. It is also important to remember that everyone's response to an injury is different. Returning to intimate experiences can be emotionally and psychologically challenging for both partners. A variety of feelings are a completely normal response and most have been experienced by others.

Suggestions for Building Intimacy

1. **Maintaining intimate relationships**: Acknowledge that after injury a romantic relationship can experience a considerable amount of stress as both partners adjust to geographic location change, possible loss of job, role and responsibility changes, and the implications of the injury. Recognize the healing benefits of romance and intimacy, and of relationships. Promote the flirtatious, sexual, and trusting side of a partnership versus the caregiving side, which is often the priority postinjury. Planning and organizing can be challenging after an injury. Even while in the hospital or soon after discharge, take turns to plan routine alone time with your partner or a date night to promote intimacy.

2. **Developing new intimate relationships**: For people who are single, finding a new partner can be exciting, but also stressful and challenging within the context of injuries. It is important to work with an OT to improve access in the community, if meeting new people, friends, and intimate partners is a challenge. Also, developing acceptance toward injuries, prompting a positive self-esteem, and demonstrating independence are helpful to attracting others. Finding a partner can vary from anonymous or random sex to wishing to develop a relationship to boyfriend/girlfriend status. Post-injury, focus sexual energy toward someone who can provide a secure, comfortable, and trusting partnership, even if that person is just a sexual friend. Friends and significant others provide an intimacy and trust level that allows for control and comfort for both partners.

3. **Developing confidence**: For both singles and those in a relationship, confidence is a huge "turn-on." Partners will likely find confidence and acceptance of injury as a strong personality trait and maybe even erotic. It is possible, after injury, that you may feel you are not capable of being a good intimate and sexual partner; or you can experience a sense of shame. These feelings will often be noticeable to a partner. Talking about these thoughts with a health care professional who addresses sexual health can alleviate self-doubts and restore confidence. You may also be pleasantly surprised and rewarded by being honest about your concerns with your partner.

4. **Affirming yourself and your partner**: Affirmation of yourself and of your partner can assist greatly with confidence. Occasionally review, either to yourself or your partner, what strengths you have that positively can contribute to a partnership. If you are in a relationship, it is equally important to affirm your partner in his or her strengths with assisting in your recovery. Take time and effort to communicate those thoughts of affirmation and show appreciation through planned intimacy dates, dates in the community, sexual dates, touch/massage, or simply saying "thanks."

5. Scheduling an intimate date: Incorporating practices that promote mutual sharing of emotions, desires, and goals can assist couples with connecting intimately. Intimate dates are one such way to strengthen connections in a relationship by reducing or eliminating distractions that take focus off the couple. An "intimate date" is defined as preplanned shared time together. It is most conducive in a private setting, such as a bedroom or living room, where the couple is alone. Setting a sensual (warm, affectionate, appealing to the senses, rather than sexual) and relaxing mood with candles, pleasant music playing, one to two drinks of alcohol (if not contraindicated by medication) or relaxing tea, and massage can all assist with creating a comfortable and open mood. The goal should be focused on conversation and nonsexual touching versus having sex or fully resolving marital issues or stressors. Keep the mood lighthearted and trusting, where both partners feel safe to share their emotions, desires, and goals in an environment where they know they will be accepted. Often, time constraints and busy schedules make setting time aside for intimacy dates challenging. It is important to plan these dates as part of your couple/family schedule, and you should try to stay dedicated to the time you have set aside. Following are suggestions for what to do or discuss during an intimacy date.

    a. Experiment with sensual massage or spend time being physically close, where touch is easy and often. This includes holding hands or stroking arms, hair, or legs.

    b. Share a favorite takeout meal or one that is easy to prepare.

    c. Tell your partner five physical attributes that attract you to him or her.

d. Tell your partner five personality attributes that attract you to him or her.

e. Share your personal and couple goals for:

i. rehabilitation

ii. parenting and/or family

iii. education or employment

iv. hobbies

v. vacations

f. "Remember when." Share past feelings, memories, or emotions when you and your partner felt happy and close.

g. Discuss where your next date or your next vacation will be.

CHAPTER 4

GENERAL TIPS FOR ENGAGING IN SEXUAL ACTIVITY

Figure 1

t is important to understand that sexual activities and pleasure will be possible regardless of injury. Where there is no
specific order of considerations prior to engaging in sex, in
this chapter might help make engaging in sex more comfortable and enjoyable.

1. **Erogenous zones**: Explore how touching any hypersensitive or hyposensitive areas and other pleasurable areas
   feels in order to start becoming comfortable in engaging/
   reengaging in intimate acts. If genitals are hypersensitive,
   amputated, or lack sensation, there may be other areas that
   could provide more pleasure now than before injury (e.g.,
   nipples, neck, ears, prostate, rectum, etc.).

2. **Body awareness**: Consider how injuries might allow for new sexual acts that were not previously possible.

   a. Increased ease of switching positions—for example, shorter lower limbs would make it easier to switch from being on top (with legs behind) into a sitting position (with legs in front)

   b. Entirely new positions

   c. New locations such as wheelchairs, shower chairs, or bathtubs, as well as locations that would now be easier to access due to resulting injuries. Be creative!

   d. Incorporation of a residual limb in creative ways, such as stimulating a female partner's clitoris with a residual limb (arm or leg)

   e. Masturbation is often the first experience with sex after a serious injury and is a great way to learn about pleasure areas. It is often used to find out if pleasure, maintained erection, ejaculation and orgasm are still possible. If you discover a loss or change in your genital sensations, or that stimulation doesn't lead to orgasm or ejaculation, your initial response may be discouragement. Don't give up! This is not a barometer of your sexual future. With proper guidance and time for healing you can discover slightly new techniques for experiencing pleasure and orgasm. These new techniques can then be taught to a partner.

3. **Desensitization**: Consider the importance of desensitizing certain areas.

  a. The ends of residual limbs, which can eventually tolerate weight bearing in multiple sexual positions (similar to increasing tolerance of walking on prosthetics)

  b. Areas of the body experiencing nerve pain or phantom limb pain: legs, arms, genitals

  c. Complete scar massage as soon as cleared by a health care provider, usually once stitches are removed. Scars causing limitations to sexual activity can be located on limbs, genitals, abdomen or face and can result in pain, decreased sensation, limited range of motion and body image concerns. General scar massage practices include rubbing the scar with oil-based lubricants; however, it is suggested to engage in scar massage only after education from your occupational therapist.

4. **Lubricants**: Consider including use of lubricants in your sexual habits for increased comfort and pleasure. Couples use lubricants for a variety of reasons: allowing for prolonged sexual experiences, assisting with self-lubrication if this is difficult for a female partner, and assisting with anal stimulation.

  a. Non-flavored water-based lubricants are considered the best option.

   i. flavored lubricants will have sugars that can cause irritations to a female partner

   ii. water-based lubricants are the easiest to clean up and typically do not leave stains

b. Oil-base lubricants are great for incorporating scar massage into your sex play.

    i. oil-based lubricants are not appropriate with use of a condom; they will damage the condom

    ii. oil-based lubricants are typically difficult to clean up, so laying a towel down prior to sex-play can be helpful.

5. **Safety**: Be attuned to changes in skin integrity, pain response, and sensation that could pose risks as you engage in sexual activity.

a. Avoid prolonged positions that may cause skin friction on areas of the body where skin irritations, breakdowns, or pressure sores are present to prevent further damage.

b. Use caution with insertion, manipulation, or use of sexual aids in or around areas of the body where diminished sensation is present.

c. Pay attention to other signs of discomfort (pounding headaches, nausea, slowed pulse, or other) when pain receptors are diminished, and stop activity and speak with your health care provider.

6. **Nonintercourse activities**: Engage in intimate and non-intimate experiences to discover abilities, concerns, and pleasure zones prior to engaging in sex. For example, oral sex positions and satisfaction, personally touching areas of injury, masturbating, massaging a partner, sensually washing a partner's body and/or genital areas, kissing a partner, and practicing specific positions during routine exercise or physical therapy (such as bridging, pushups, or use of bolsters) can lead to greater awareness of pleasure and abilities.

7. **Communication**: Communicate your needs and ideas with your partner. Certain topics to discuss before sexual engagement might be:

   a. Whether to use a sex toy or positioning aide
   b. Different positions
   c. Different locations
   d. Whether to wear prosthetics
   e. What does and does not feel good for your partner to provide stimulation either via touch, orally, with a device, or during intercourse. This can be learned through self-exploration of erogenous zones and improving awareness of your own body.

8. **Expectations**: Discuss expectations for intimate relations to provide opportunities for partners to align expectations and ensure they are realistic. Discuss expectations and assumptions with a health care provider to enlighten service members and loved ones regarding the legitimacy of assumptions or the realistic nature of expectations. Lastly, focus expectations with yourself or your partner on a pleasurable and erotic sexual experience, versus a demanding one, where one or both partners have to orgasm. This may to be more effective in enjoying positive sexual experiences, enhancing confidence, and increasing the likelihood of repetition.

9. **Planned sex is not boring sex**: Throughout the manual, planned sexual activities are suggested multiple times; however, it is important to highlight that "planned" does not mean predictable or boring. Planning is important for child care management, scheduling around high energy and low pain times, managing bowel and bladder needs, and preparing equipment if necessary. What happens during

that planned encounter can still be unpredictable, leading to increased desire, anticipation, and eroticism. Both partners can think about how they will add excitement to the planned sexual encounter, for example, with a new technique, role play idea, sex toys, music, candles and aromas, or lingerie.

10. **Bowel and bladder management**: Understand that sexual activities can still take place while catheters and ostomy bags are attached to the body. Plan for sexual activity after bowel and bladder routines have been completed, such as, the emptying of ostomy and urine bags. Communication with a partner and self-questioning can identify comfort level with bags. Consider using a towel to cover the ostomy bag or catheter and using scented candles or massage lotion to enhance sensual smells.

11. **Medication management**: Discuss challenges caused by medications with health care providers and partners. Medications to manage the milieu of medical needs after injury can result in decreased sexual desire, increased fatigue, difficulty gaining or sustaining an erection, and difficulty ejaculating. Your health care provider can provide education and discuss options. Consider exploring other erogenous zones during sexual activity to enhance the experience; increasing desire through flirtation, romance, and foreplay; and planning sexual activity during times of the day or night when one is most rested.

CHAPTER 5

MODIFICATIONS & ADAPTATIONS

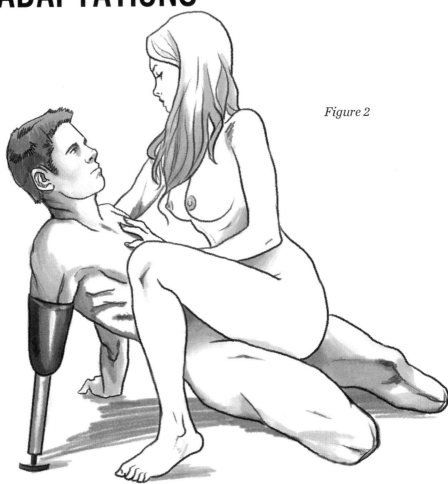

Figure 2

As is the case with many other physical activities, the use of modifications and adaptations can help facilitate sexual activity when you are ready to engage in intimacy with your partner. Occupational therapists are specifically trained in making adaptations and modifications to allow patients to complete everyday activities, including sexual activity, based on a task analysis. During an activity analysis, an OT will break down an activity and identify the difficulty in performing the tasks. Modifications and adaptations can then be found to compensate for the difficulty. Sometimes the solutions are universal and common items, whereas other solutions may be individually customized. Often patients are their own best problem solvers, and occupational therapists can assist with encouraging creativity and an open mind, as well as suggesting solutions. Many of the devices listed in this manual can be combined to achieve a variety of solutions.

What works for one individual may not work for another because injuries and their effects differ. Below are a variety of sexual positioning aids, equipment, and devices. These can be used individually or combined to achieve various activities or positions. The products listed can be purchased through multiple websites for varying prices. This list is not all-inclusive, and there are many versions of similar devices/ equipment available that may be better for each individual. These products are not endorsed by the authors but are merely recommendations. Of utmost importance is to clean your sexual device with strict accordance to the direction from the manufacturer. This is to ensure proper hygiene of the device, which will impact the hygiene of your skin and decrease the risk of infection.

Adaptive Devices

Universal Cuff or Residual Limb Cuffs

A **universal cuff** (❶) is a cuff placed on a hand/residual limb into which various items can be inserted, such as a toothbrush or fork. Sexual assistance devices (e.g., massagers, vibrators, dildos) can be modified to be attached to a universal cuff so that the individual can manipulate that device effectively. A **residual limb cuff** is a customized cuff that is attached to the residual limb and can be used in a similar fashion to the universal cuff.

Mounting systems: Gooseneck Clamps/Stands, Suction Cups

Gooseneck clamps or stands (❺) can be fixed to stable surfaces, such as grab bars, and devices can be attached to them. For example, a vibrator or "masturbation sleeve" can be attached for hands-free use. The length and flexibility of these goosenecks can vary, which can be helpful depending on what is needed. Suction cups are helpful for stabilizing devices to allow for hands-free use. There are suction cups in the form of hooks, handles, or clamps.

Hand Orthoses/Splints

A **hand orthosis or splint** (❷) provides stability or grasp assistance and can be custom-made or store-bought. Devices can be attached to these in a variety of ways.

Prosthetics

Upper and lower prosthetics (❸) can be worn during sexual activities, depending on comfort level or level of assist needed. Prosthetics can also be designed for specific activities. For example, a leg or arm prosthetic could be adapted to hold a device or fabricated to assist with positioning. There are also terminal devices that can be used for weight bearing through an arm or for grasping certain items. See Figure 2.

Bathroom adaptations (❹) such as grab bars, shower chairs, and tub benches can provide new opportunities for satisfying sex positions. A shower assists with providing a relaxing and comfortable environment to assist with initiation and increasing pleasure. A shower chair or tub bench allows for seated sexual activities in a variety of ways. For example, being seated on shower chair allows for sufficient postural support and allows the seated individual to use his or her hands. Grabs bars assist with standing and balance, leverage for thrusting, and overall stability, as well as locations for attaching sexual devices for hands-free use. A wheelchair, in which the arm rests/lateral supports can be removed, allows for seated sexual activities or positions in which a partner is to be straddled. See Figure 3.

Positioning Aids

⑥ ⑦ ⑧ Liberator Pillows

$90 and up / www.liberator.com / Removable and washable cover

- Evens out height for residual limbs, matches partners' pelvis heights, allows deeper penetration, provides a higher surface on which to rest arms.
- Assists with oral sex positioning
- Company website provides position suggestions for each type of liberator. See Figure 1.

⑪ ⑫ ⑬ Love Bumper

$90 and up / www.lovebumper.com / Removable and washable covers

- Evens out height for residual limbs, matching partners' pelvis heights, allowing deeper penetration, provides a higher surface to rest arms on.
- Assists with oral sex positioning
- Company website provides position suggestions for each type of bumper.

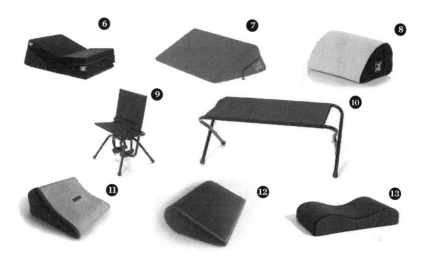

❾ ❿ IntimateRider

www.intimaterider.com (Available at multiple online stores) / $365 for IntimateRider / $150 for RiderMate / Cleanable

- IntimateRider seat glides to assist with thrusting.
- RiderMate allows for partners to be in various positions and provides surface for upper body support of the partner seated on the intimate rider.
- Reduces fatigue for both partners, depending on position, and eases thrust if mobility is decreased.
- Company website provides position suggestions.

Sexual Equipment and Devices

1. Masturbation Sleeves

⑭ a. Tenga Flip

$100 / www.tenga-global.com / www.amazon.com (Available at multiple online stores) / Company website helps guide consumer to choose products based on specific needs
- Reusable and cleanable
- 4 colors
- Open, apply lubricant, insert penis, and close top/bottom

Suggested Use
- Allows for masturbation by simulating penetration; some offer vibration/textures.
- Tenga Flip has hard outer cover that could be grasped by a prosthetic.
- Helpful for those with weak grasp, hemiparises, nerve injuries, partial hand amputations and upper extremity amputations to allow for grasp free or hands-free use.
  *see adaptations section for ways to adapt these types of items

2. *Vibrators*

⑮ a. Magic Remote Bullet

$30 / www.comeasyouare.com
- Allows vibration to be controlled from a remote.
- Helpful for those with weak grasp, hemiparises, nerve injuries, partial hand amputations and upper extremity amputations.

⑯⑰ b. Tongue Joy

$19.95 / www.tonguejoy.com/
- Enhances oral sex for either partner.
- Helpful for those with weak grasp, hemiparises, nerve injuries, partial hand amputations and upper extremity amputations.

⑱ c. Wahl massager

$50-70 / www.cvs.com / www.adamandeve.com
- Can be used for body massage as well as stimulating either partner's genitals.
- Has multiple attachments.
- Some have heating options.
- Helpful for those with weak grasp, hemiparises, nerve injuries, partial hand amputations and upper extremity amputations.

⑲ d. Hitachi Massagers

$30-60 / www.amazon.com
- Can be used for body massage as well as stimulating either partners genitals
- Has multiple attachments
- Helpful for those with weak grasp, hemiparises, nerve injuries, partial hand amputations and upper extremity amputations

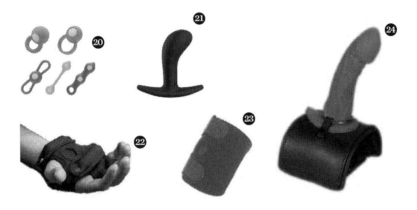

㉚ e. Vi-Bo by Tenga

www.tenga-global.com
- Five different devices to allow for multi-use stimulation through vibration

Features:
- 2 fingers free vibrators
- 1 penis vibrator which also provide stimulation to clitoris
- Great for encouraging creativity

Helpful for those with:
- Weak grasp, amputated fingers, decreased fine motor
- Genital nerve injuries, genital amputations, genital sensitivity or pain issue
- Desire to explore different sensations for multiple erogenous zones.

f. We Vibe
$50-$75 / www.amazon.com
- Provides vibration stimulation to both partners during intercourse. The toy is inserted into female prior to penis insertion, thus stimulating both internally and externally for females, and the penis inside the vagina for males.

– This device adds girth to penis, which can be helpful for those with genital injuries.

㉑ g. Anal Vibrators

$30-60 / www.comeasyouare.com / www.adamandeve.com
- Some are dildos, some vibrators depending on stimulation needs.
- Can be used externally or internally depending on person's interest and comfort levels to provide alternative stimulation options to prostate and anus
- Helpful for those with genital amputations, genital nerve injuries, or genital sensitivity or pain issues.

3. *Other devices*

㉒ a. Spare Parts La Palma Hand Harness

$110 / www.comeasyouare.com / Neoprene, waterproof, easily cleaned
- Glove allows dildo/vibrator to be attached and used by either partner.
- Helpful for those with genital injuries/dysfunction, weak grasp, limited mobility.

b. Strap-ons/men's harness

- Allows dildo to be strapped onto either partner. Men's harness allows for men with intact genitalis to still use strap-on but protect that area.
- Allows partners to be physically close for intimacy.
- Helpful for those with genital injuries/dysfunction.

c. Thigh Riders

㉓ Neoprene thigh harness: $40 /
www.comeasyouare.com

㉔ Sinvention Thigh Harness: $90 /
www.comeasyouare.com

– Allows dildo or vibrator to be strapped onto thigh.
– Allows partners to be physically close for intimacy.
– Helpful for those with genital injuries/dysfunc-
tion, and those with limited mobility for physical
or neurological reasons.

Figure 3

CHAPTER 6

SEXUAL POSITIONING

Figure 5

After a traumatic injury, positioning for sexual activities may be affected. As there are a variety of orthopedic/ neurological injuries, there are no universal or specific recommendations for positioning that work for everyone or every specific injury. Determining successful positions for you and your partner involves creative problem solving, using positioning aids, and communicating with your partner and health care providers. It is important to keep in mind this is a gradual process and trial and error may be necessary. Provided below are general positioning tips, and then specific positioning tips for those with neurologic-based mobility impairments and those who have amputations. The tips are not meant to be all-inclusive of techniques for specific positions or inclusive of all positions available.

General Positioning Tips

When it comes to successful positioning, experiment with positions and positioning aids that provide both partners with a sufficient level of physical and psychological ease. Talk through and respect any hesitations.

1. Consider comfortable, nonfatiguing positions, such as lying on your side, lying down, or being seated.
2. Use pillows to position limbs or lower back.
3. Incorporate equipment that you currently have, such as a wheelchair, or shower chair/bench.
4. Ask health care providers such as OT/PT for positioning suggestions.

Neurological-based Mobility Impairments Positioning Tips

Traumatic brain injuries, strokes, and spinal cord injuries may result in neurological mobility impairments such as mono- (one limb), para- (two limbs), hemi- (arm and leg on right or left side of body), quadra- (all four limbs) paresis, the weakness or partial loss of voluntary movement, or plegia, the complete paralysis of limbs. The following positioning tips are offered as a starting place to support or enhance sexual activity under these conditions.

1. Limited Arm Movement
   a. Consider bearing weight through forearm. See Figure 1.
   b. Have your partner assist with the placement and/or stabilization of limb.
   c. See the Sexual Equipment and Devices section for items that can be used in place of using hand for partner or self-stimulation.
   d. See the Modifications and Adaptions section to identify ways to affix toy to arm or to use toy arm- or hands-free.

Figure 4

2. No Arm Movement

   a. Consider using pillows to support limb comfortably.

   b. Decide whether an arm sling could better support and protect limb during sexual activities.

   c. See the Sexual Equipment and Devices section for items that could be used in place of using your hand for partner or self-stimulation.

   d. See the Modifications and Adaptions section for ways to affix toy to arm or use toy arm- or hands-free.

3. Limited Leg Movement

   a. Consider seated positions to compensate for difficulty standing or kneeling.

   b. See the Positioning Aids section for aids that can support limb or body and allow for increase mobility.

   c. Consider a seated position on a mattress to allow for ideal use of abdominals to thrust with spring of mattress assisting.

   d. Consider weight bearing through the stronger limb and using both hands on a walker to support yourself when standing and generating forward motion of the pelvis. See Figure 5.

4. No Leg Movement

   a. Consider seated positions to compensate for difficulty in standing or kneeling.

   b. See the Positioning Aids section for aids that can allow for increased mobility.

   c. Consider a seated position on a mattress to allow for ideal use of abdominals to thrust with spring of mattress assisting.

   d. If not able to bear weight through limb secondary to orthopedic injuries or unable to support weight of body with limb secondary to nerve injuries, consider using a walker to support self in standing. See Figure 5.

Positioning Considerations for Amputee Population

These suggestions are not meant to be all-inclusive of techniques for the specific positions or all-inclusive of the positions available to the amputee population. People are only limited by their own imaginations. Also, while this list identifies a "couple" as comprising members of opposite sexes, and identifies the injured partner as male, many of these suggestions can be used and applied to same-sex couples, as well as females who are amputees.

Figure 6

1. Single BKA/AKA

Male on top
Use knees to assist with thrusting and hands to support self on top. If AKA, female can place her hand or leg on back of male's leg as support to thrust against. See Figure 1.

Doggy style
In kneeling position, use knees and hands (either on bed or partner's back) to provide support. Consider wearing prosthetics if kneeling balance is challenging, or using a pillow or wedge underneath an AKA side to level out kneeling balance. See Figure 6.

Male siting up
Use hands and arms to assist with her up-down thrust, or consider kneeling and leaning back with hands on the bed, to allow for pelvic thrusting. See Figure 2.

Female on top
Male partner can use remaining foot to thrust upwards. Consider placing small bolster under residual limb to push up on (similar to bridging), or angle female's lower leg and place residual limb over female's calf to assist with increasing thrusting upward. See Figure 4.

2. Bilateral BKA

Male on top
Similar to Single BKA/AKA, consider wearing prosthetics if balance on your knees is challenging. See Figure 1.

Doggy style
Similar to Single BKA/AKA, consider wearing prosthetics if kneeling balance is challenging. A pillow or wedge can assist holding female partner at similar height/angle, or consider standing. See Figure 6.

Male siting up
Similar to Single BKA/AKA. See Figure 2.

Female on top
Consider placing small bolster under residual limb to push up on (similar to bridging), or angle female's lower leg and place residual limb over female's calf to assist with increasing thrusting upwards. See Figure 4.

3. Bilateral AKA

Male on top
After sufficient desensitization of residual limb, attain position and thrust with increased core use and hand support. The female partner can assist by stabilizing the back of the residual limb with her hands or with use of her lower legs to prevent the residual limbs from sliding back. This may provide leverage for the male to thrust. Considering limb length, you might be able to shift between positions without withdrawing (such as Male on top to sitting upright). Consider using a pillow/wedge to support female's pelvis at a raised height to allow for easier/increased penetration. See Figure 1.

Doggy style
After sufficient desensitization of residual limb, attain position and thrust with increased core use and hand support. Consider wearing prosthetics and stand up as alternate option if possible. Consider using a pillow to support female's pelvis at a raised height to allow for easier/increased penetration. See Figure 6.

Male siting up
Thrust up with primary use of arms on bed and pushing down into bed with end of residual limbs to thrust pelvis upward (similar to bridging). Spring in mattress will assist with thrusting. See Figure 2.

Female on top
Similar to Bilateral BKA. See Figure 4.

4. Unilateral Hip Disarticulation/ Hemipelvectomy (combined with a fully intact leg on the other side, an BKA, or AKA)

Male on top
Consider using a pillow/bolster as a surface for the area of the hip disarticulation or hemipelvectomy to rest on to level out the other side of the pelvis. Place partner on wedge, and while on top of her, use forearms on wedge to assist with thrust. Partner can assist with maintaining your balance on top.

Doggy style
Consider using a pillow/bolster as a surface for the area of the hip disarticulation or hemipelvectomy to rest on, to level out kneeling or other residual limb height on the bed. Prosthetics are also an option to level out kneeling height and allow for genitals to be accessed.

Male siting up
Similar to Bilateral AKA. If the other side is a fully intact leg, then bending the knee will give a wide base of a support and also will allow for some leverage for potential thrusting.

Female on top
Similar to Bilateral AKA. See Figure 4.

5. Bilateral Hip Disarticulation/Hemipelvectomy

Male on top
Consider using a pillow/bolster as a surface for the area of hip disarticulation or hemipelvectomy to rest on, to level male and female pelvises to allow for penetration. Lean forward and use core and arms to assist with thrust. Place partner on wedge, and while on top of her, use forearms on wedge to assist with thrust. Partner can assist with maintaining your balance on top.

Doggy style
The female can lie on her stomach (use of a pillow or towel roll under her pelvis optional) with male partner on top and behind her, using core/arms to assist with thrust. Alternately, if male partner is seated in a chair or wheelchair, female can backward straddle and thrust up and down.

Male siting up
With female partner straddling in kneeling position and facing male partner, use hands and arms to assist with her up/down movement.

Female on top
The male partner can use his hands to pleasure her or to assist with stabilizing his trunk by holding on or pushing against headboard or side of bed.

6. Unilateral upper extremity amputee

Male on top
Use a wedge to help shorten the distance between arm and the bed. Consider using mushroom prosthetic against bed to assist with thrusting forward. See Figure 1.

Doggy style
Consider using a prosthetic against bed to assist with thrusting. Use a wedge to help shorten distance between arm and the bed.

Male siting up
Consider using mushroom prosthetic against bed to assist with thrusting up. See Figure 2.

Female on top
No modification needed. Consider lightly stimulating her nipples with your residual limb or attaching feather or other stimulating tool to your residual limb with a universal cuff.

7. Bilateral upper extremity amputee

Male on top
Similar to Unilateral upper extremity amputee. See Figure 1.

Doggy style
Similar to above. It may help to have one arm on the head of the bed and one arm supporting on the bed. Alternately, the female can lie on her stomach (pillow or roll under her pelvis optional) with male partner lying on top behind her, using core/arms to assist with thrust. Another option has the male partner seated with female reverse straddling.

Male siting up
Use prosthetics to stabilize yourself while seated, or use residual limb under partner's arms to assist her in thrusting up and down. See Figure 2.

Female on top
No modification needed. Consider lightly stimulating her nipples with your residual limb or attaching feather or other stimulating tool to your residual limb with a universal cuff.

8. Triple amputee

Male on top
Similar to bilateral AKA/BKA/ Hip or unilateral upper extremity amputee. See Figure 1.

Doggy style
Similar to bilateral AKA/BKA/Hip or unilateral upper extremity amputee. Consider wearing lower limb prosthetics and do while standing. See Figure 6.

Male siting up
Similar to bilateral AKA/BKA/Hip or unilateral upper extremity amputee. Consider using prosthetic against bed to assist with thrusting up with assist from spring in bed. See Figure 2.

Female on top
Similar to bilateral AKA/BKA/Hip or unilateral upper extremity amputee. See Figure 4.

9. Quadruple amputee

Male on top
Use similar techniques as Bilateral AKA/BKA/Hip/ Hemi or Bilateral upper extremity. Consider using prosthetics to assist with either upper or lower extremities. See Figure 1.

Doggy style
Use similar techniques as Bilateral AKA/BKA/Hip/Hemi or Bilateral upper extremity. Consider using prosthetics to assist with either upper or lower extremities. See Figure 6.

Male siting up
Use similar techniques as Bilateral AKA/BKA/Hip/Hemi or Bilateral upper extremity. Consider using prosthetics to assist with either upper or lower extremities. See Figure 2.

Female on top
Use similar techniques as Bilateral AKA/BKA/Hip or Bilateral upper extremity amputee. See Figure 4.

RESOURCES YOU MAY BE INTERESTED TO KNOW ABOUT

Barry McCarthy and Emily McCarthy, *Sexual Awareness: Your Guide to Healthy Couple Sexuality*, 5th ed. (New York: Routledge, 2012). http://psychcentral.com/lib/sexual-awareness-your-guide-to-healthy-couple-sexuality/00012164.

Sallie Foley, Sally A. Kope, and Dennis P. Sugrue, S*ex Matters for Women, A Complete Guide to Taking Care of Your Sexual Self*, 2nd ed. (New York: The Guilford Press, 2011). http://www.amazon.com/Sex-Matters-Women-Second-Edition/dp/1609184696.

Ken Kroll and Erica Levy Klein, *Enabling Romance: A Guide to Love, Sex and Relationships for People with Disabilities (and the People who Care About Them)* (Horsham, PA: No Limits Communications, 2001). http://www.amazon.com/Enabling-Romance-Relationships-People-Disabilities/dp/0971284202.

Kate Naphtali, Edith MacHattie, Stacy L. Elliott, *Pleasure Able, Sexual Device Manual for Persons with Disabilities* (Vancouver, BC: Disabilities Health Research Network, 2009). http://www.dhrn.ca/files/sexualhealthmanual_lowres_2010_0208.pdf.

ACKNOWLEDGEMENTS

The authors want to extend their sincere gratitude to the many people who inspired and shaped not only this manual but our approach to patient care. Too many to single out, we thank our family members, leaders, peers, and patients.

A huge thank you, also, to

 and

For their generous support and funding for this manual.

The Bob Woodruff Foundation (BWF) is the nonprofit organization dedicated to ensuring injured service members and their families are thriving long after they return home. A national organization with grassroots reach, the Bob Woodruff Foundation complements the work of the federal government—diligently navigating the maze of more than 46,000 nonprofits providing services to veterans—finds, funds and shapes innovative programs, and holds them accountable for results. To date, BWF has invested more than $25 million in public education and solutions, reaching more than 2 million service members, support personnel, veterans and their families. The Bob Woodruff Foundation was co-founded in 2006 by award-winning anchor Bob Woodruff and his family, whose own experiences inspired them to help make sure the nation's heroes have access to the high level of support and resources they deserve, for as long as they need it. For more information about the Bob Woodruff Foundation, please visit bobwoodrufffoundation.org.

SemperMax Support Fund works to enhance morale and welfare of service disabled veterans and their families through the support of a team, in the hope of reducing isolation, disenfranchisement from society, and suicide among veterans and their family members. SemperMax Support Fund is a civilian organization with 501(c)(3) status, is not a government agency, and is supported by the generosity of individuals, corporations, and foundations committed to the welfare of our nation's wounded heroes. Federal Tax ID#27-1063578. For more information about SemperMax, visit www.sempermax.org.

Design, layout, editing, programming and consulting provided by The Sager Group LLC. For more information please visit www.TheSagerGroup.net.

ABOUT THE AUTHORS

Kathryn Ellis and Caitlin Dennison live and practice occupational therapy in the Washington, D.C. area, with a specialty serving military service members. Kathryn is originally from Newark, Delaware. She went to James Madison University for her undergraduate degree and master's degree in occupational therapy. Caitlin is originally from Pompton Lakes, New Jersey. She attended The College of New Jersey for her undergraduate degree and Columbia University for her master's degree in occupational therapy. To contact the authors, please email: otkathrynellis@gmail.com.

Made in the USA
Middletown, DE
22 January 2023

21919159R00040